DMITRI
Kabalevsky
24 PIECES FOR CHILDREN Op.39
for Piano

G. SCHIRMER, *Inc.*

DISTRIBUTED BY
HAL•LEONARD®
CORPORATION
7777 W. BLUEMOUND RD. P.O. BOX 13819 MILWAUKEE, WI 53213

ED. 2461

24 Pieces for Children

1 Melody

Dmitri Kabalevsky, Op. 39

2 Polka

3 Rambling

4 Cradle Song

5 Playing

Allegretto

6 A Little Joke

Scherzando

7 Funny Event

8 Song

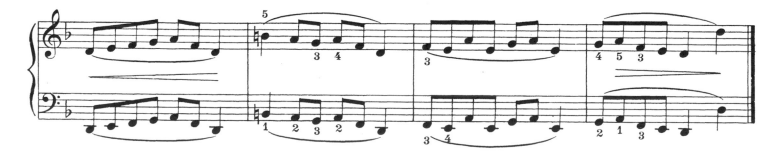

9 A Little Dance

Allegro molto

10 March

Energico

11 Song of Autumn

Andante cantabile

12 Scherzo

Vivo, giocoso

13 Waltz

Moderato

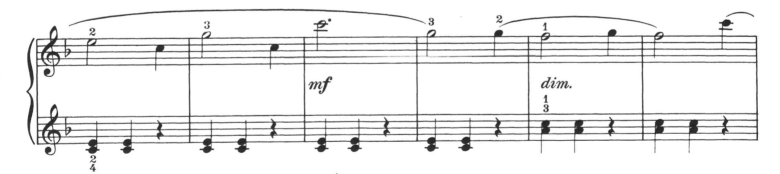

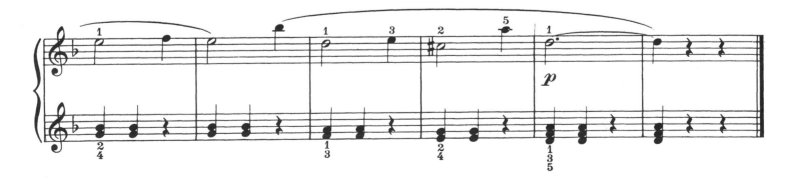

14 A Fable

15 Jumping

16 A Sad Story

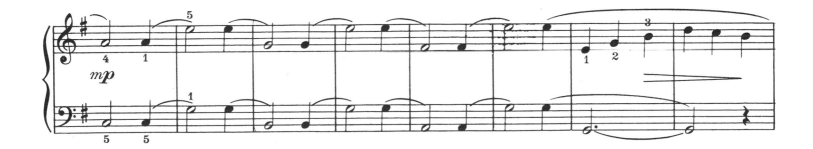

17 Folk Dance

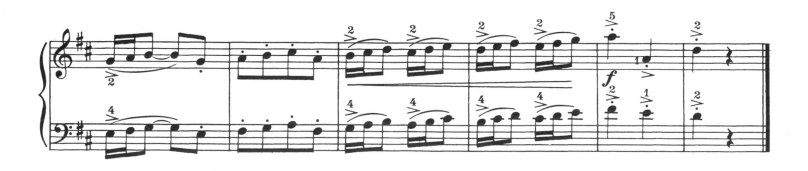

18 Galop

Animato

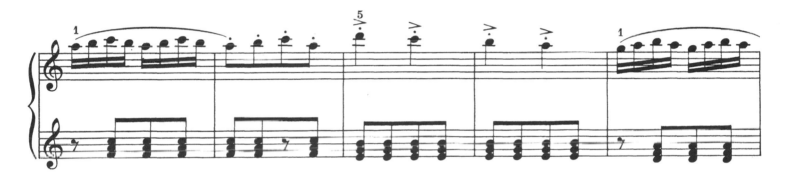

19 Prelude

Moderato

20 Clowns

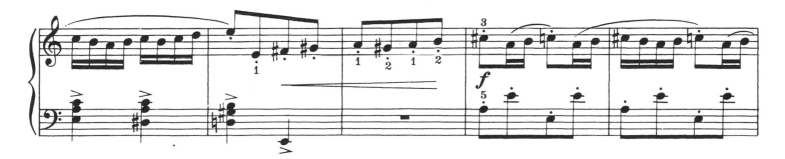

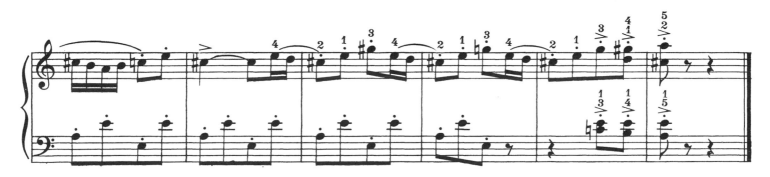

21 Improvisation

22 A Short Story

dim. poco a poco

p

pp

23 Slow Waltz

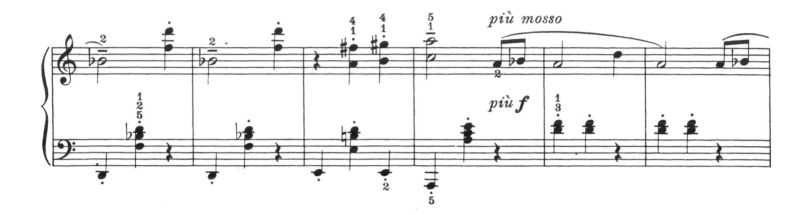

Tempo I

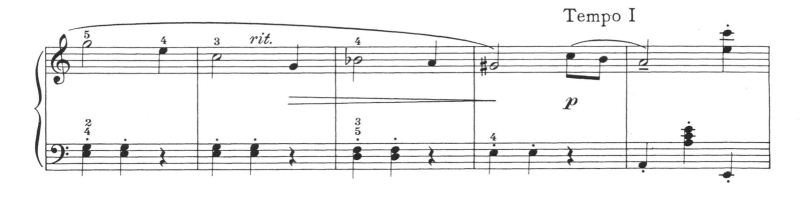

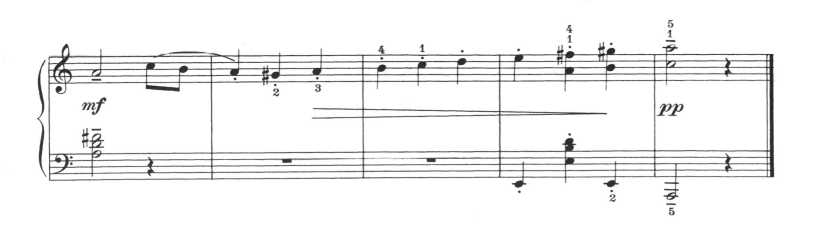

24 A Happy Outing

Resoluto con brio